50 Syncopated SNARE DRUM SOLOS

T0101618

A Modern Approach for Jazz, Pop, and Rock Drummers

By Sperie Karas

To access audio visit:
www.halleonard.com/mylibrary

Enter Code
3230-8761-7156-9661

ISBN 978-1-4803-4441-9

HAL•LEONARD® CORPORATION

7777 W. BLUEMOUND RD. P.O. BOX 13819 MILWAUKEE, WI 53213

In Australia Contact:
Hal Leonard Australia Pty. Ltd.
4 Lentara Court
Cheltenham, Victoria, 3192 Australia
Email: ausadmin@halleonard.com.au

Visit Hal Leonard Online at
www.halleonard.com

Contents

Notes from the Author

The suggested tempos are meant to be guides and can be modified.

When ♩=♪ is indicated, the eighth-note "ands" are swung—played on the third eighth of the eighth-note triplet: ♪. "Even 8ths" and all other notes are played as written.

Use alternate sticking unless otherwise marked. If you find a sticking that suits you better, use that one, as long as the music is served, and you're comfortable and relaxed!

On some of the fifty solos, I have suggested a hi-hat and bass drum accompaniment (drumset). I advise playing this accompaniment, but you can stick with the solo snare only. On the audio track, you'll notice that I play accompaniment on all of the solos although, sometimes, I only use the hi-hat, depending on what kind of "feel" I want. Begin the solos with two bars of ride rhythm "time" as I do on the audio.

The solos are played without repeats on the audio.

On pages 58–65, I have written out examples from some of the snare solos to give you an idea of how the solos can be practiced on the drumset. Pages 68–71 show comping possibilities.

The abbreviations and placement of the instruments on the drumset—the notation key—is on page 57.

And, of course, "R" is for the right hand and "L" is for the left hand.

The only thing left now is for me to wish you much success and enjoyment!

Sperie Karas

About the Author

Sperie Karas began playing drums at an early age, and continued his studies at the Juilliard School in New York. During this time he formed a group that appeared, among other venues, at the famous Birdland.

When Eddie Sauter was invited to lead the SWF Band in Baden-Baden, Germany, he asked Sperie to be his drummer.

Sperie's next big move, after a period of freelancing, was the drum chair of the WDR Big Band in Cologne, which gave him the opportunity to meet and work with many outstanding international jazz musicians such as Dizzy Gillespie, Freddie Hubbard, Tony Scott, Bill Holman, and Ernie Wilkins.

Being an educator was always an important aspect of Sperie's musical endeavors, and he still continues to be active in that field. He is the author of several books, including *Jazz Drumming in Big Band & Combo*, *Jazz Drumset Solos: 7 Contemporary Pieces*, *Snare Drum Solos: Seven Pieces for Concert Performance*, and *Rock Drumset Solos: 8 Contemporary Pieces*.

Sperie and his wife divide their time between Florida and Germany.

THE 50 Syncopated SNARE DRUM SOLOS

My goal with these fifty syncopated solos is to present a modern approach that can be applied to the contemporary music of today. In addition to regular 4/4 time, I have written solos in odd and changing meters, which will sharpen your reading abilities.

When playing these solos, always focus on the music. The lines should make sense musically; dynamics and accents are of utmost importance. Think horizontally and make the phrases flow, imparting a kind of improvised feel. A click is certainly advisable when you're first starting.

Except for the Latin solos (36 and 41), I have demonstrated the solos on the audio with a jazz feel—swung eighths—which I indicate at the top of each solo. You can also play these solos using straight eighth notes, with a pop/rock feeling. In this case, start the solos with two bars of rock groove. The bass drum and hi-hat can be played as I indicate, or in a way that makes you feel comfortable playing the piece.

The same applies to the second and third sections of this book, Snare Drum Solos on the Drumset and Comping Snare Drum Solos. My original concept is with the jazz feel, as you hear on the audio, but you can use the rock approach with straight eighths, starting with two bars of rock groove. In the third section, I would play the ride cymbal with straight eighths.

Always keep that moving jazz feel in mind when playing these solos and make them swing, and if you go the rock route, make them groove!

SOLO 1

Note the hi-hat at letter A, and the hi-hat and bass drum at letter B when playing this 4/4 piece on the drumset.

SOLO 2

Swing the eighth notes and don't forget to play the hi-hat, or the bass drum and hi-hat on the drumset, as in Solo 1.

SOLO 3

SOLO 4

Medium Jazz ♩ = ca. 124

SOLO 5

SOLO 6

SOLO 7

Medium fast Jazz ♩ = ca. 138

SOLO 8

Also try playing the hi-hat on all four quarter notes, as shown in the first four bars of letter A.

SOLO 9

SOLO 10

SOLO 11

SOLO 12

For more of a "two feeling," play the hi-hat and bass drum as shown in the first four bars of letter A.

SOLO 13

Only the eighth-note "ands" are played with a jazz feeling. All other notes are played as written.

SOLO 14

SOLO 15

Keep the hi-hat and bass drum in mind when using the drumset! Note the first four bars of letter A.

SOLO 16

SOLO 17

SOLO 18

SOLO 20

Medium fast Jazz ♩ = ca. 142

SOLO 21

Look at letter A for the hi-hat and bass drum when playing the drumset.

SOLO 22

Try playing the hi-hat on beats 2 and 3, as shown at letter A.

SOLO 23

On the set, try playing the hi-hat as shown at letter A.

Medium fast Jazz Waltz ♩ = ca. 142

SOLO 24

SOLO 25

Try playing the bass drum and hi-hat as in the first four bars of letter A.

SOLO 26

SOLO 27

SOLO 28

On the drumset, try playing the hi-hat and bass drum as shown at A.

SOLO 29

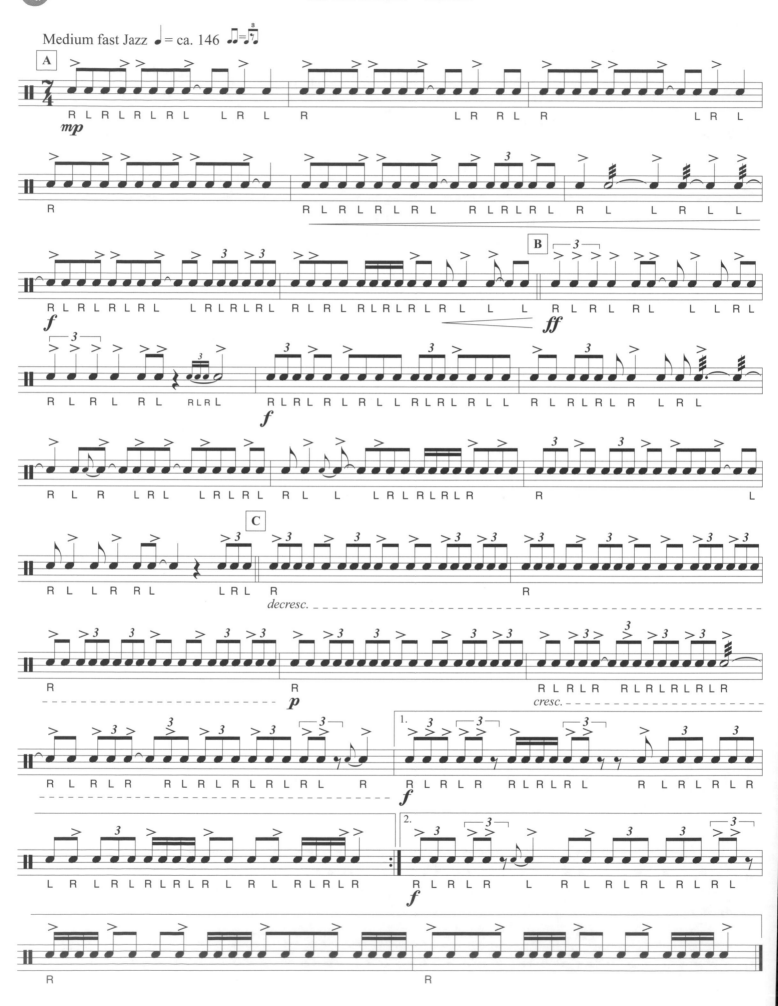

SOLO 30

Observe the first bar in A for the hi-hat and bass drum, and the first bar in B for just the hi-hat on the drumset.

The hi-hat and bass drum can be played as shown in the first two bars of A.

SOLO 32

Note the first bar of A and B for the hi-hat and bass drum.

SOLO 33

Fast Jazz ♩ = ca. 200

SOLO 34

Two different suggestions for the hi-hat and bass drum are found in the first bar of A and the first bar of B. In up-tempo sections, the eighths take on more of a straight feel.

SOLO 35

Medium Jazz ♩ = ca. 126

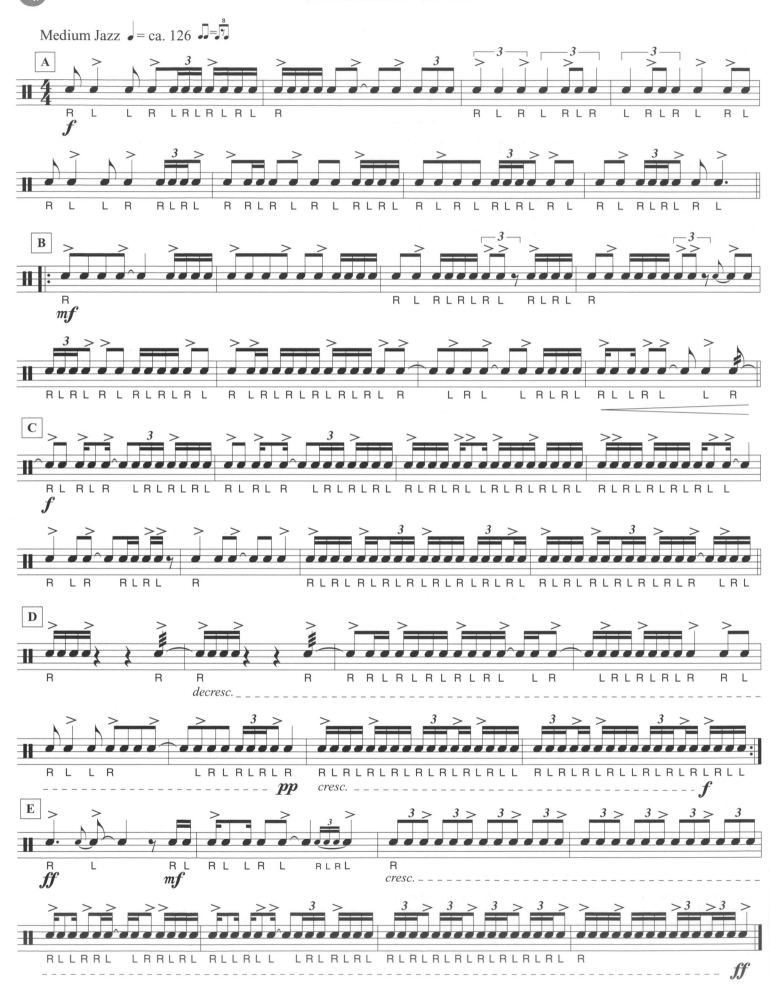

40

SOLO 36

For the Latin sections, note how the bass drum and hi-hat are played, using a "2 feel," in the first four bars of A; for the swing sections, which have a "4 feel," see the first bar of C. Play even eighths in the Latin sections and jazz eighths in the swing sections.

SOLO 37

On this piece, try playing the hi-hat on quarter notes.

SOLO 38

As with solo 34, the faster tempos require straight eighths.

SOLO 39

Don't forget to play the hi-hat, or the hi-hat and bass drum, when using the drumset!

SOLO 40

SOLO 41

Play even eighths in the Latin sections and jazz eighths in the swing sections. Look at the first four bars of A and the first bar of B for the bass drum and hi-hat when using the drumset.

SOLO 42

SOLO 44

Here, again, we play straight eighths in the up-tempo sections.

SOLO 45

See the first bar of each time signature change for bass drum and hi-hat ideas on drumset.

SOLO 46

SOLO 47

SOLO 48

SOLO 49

SOLO 50

Medium slow Jazz ♩ = ca. 100

SNARE DRUM SOLOS ON THE DRUMSET

As I mentioned in the Notes from the Author, these snare drum solos lend themselves extremely well for the drumset.

Use the examples I have given on the following pages, with their comments, to learn how you might orchestrate the fifty syncopated snare drum solos on the drumset. Always look for different ways to distribute the notes. Be imaginative with the sound and colors when applying the solos to the drumset. I have only given you a beginning look; you will soon discover the vast possibilities that present themselves when you begin to experiment. Constantly search for different solutions; e.g., if you have just played a lick on the snare, play it the next time on the high (mounted) tom, or between the high tom and floor (low) tom. Change the sequence of the instruments the next time! Perhaps begin on the floor tom. You'll be amazed at how many different sounding phrases and licks you'll come up with!

If you need to adjust the tempos, or sometimes sticking, to achieve the musical results you're aiming for, do so. The main thing is to make the phrases and licks swing and groove.

In the next section, on pages 68–71, I'll discuss the area of comping the snare drum solos.

You have noticed on the demo audio that I start all of the examples with ride rhythm, and I strongly suggest you do also.

Notation Key

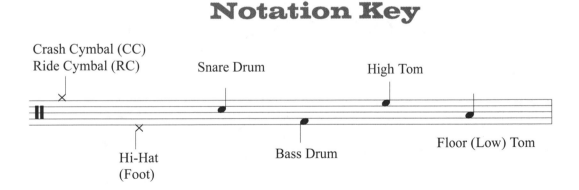

SOLO 12, LETTER C

On this first example of playing syncopated snare drum solos on the drumset, I have presented both the original eight-bar excerpt from Solo 12, letter C, and the same eight bars written for drumset. You have an immediate comparison. This will only be done on this first example. Also on this first drumset part, I have indicated the instruments to be played, which I discontinue in the following examples. If you need, refer to the notation key on page 57.

The tempo is ♩ = ca. 142, but feel free to begin at a slower tempo. When you have seen how I have played these bars on the drumset, use that as a guide to go back and do the entire Solo 12 on the drumset. This should start you on your way to playing the other snare drum solos on the set. And the next examples on pages 59– 65 will further aid you in orchestrating the snare drum solos on the drumset. Have fun!

As I do on the demo track, start with ride rhythm!

SOLO 12, LETTER C
as It Could Be Played on the Drumset

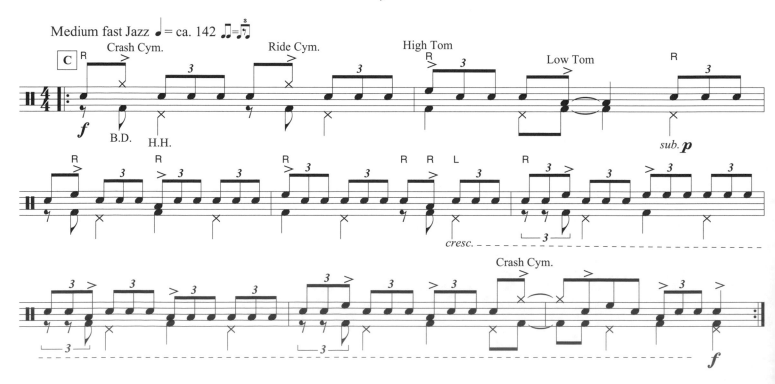

SOLO 20, LETTER C

All kinds of orchestration possibilities present themselves here, especially with the sixteenth notes. This example is only one of them.

SOLO 24, LETTER F

Here I've sketched out my approach to letter F. Use this as a guide and do the whole solo on the drumset.

SOLO 25, LETTER C

On this example, I tried to capture the flowing feeling of 5/4 time. This kind of training can be a big help with your accompanying and solo work in ensembles.

SOLO 28, LETTER D

7/4 is certainly a challenge, but as you have seen with the snare drum, once you have the right feel, it is as natural as 4/4 time. This is how I might play this phrase on the drumset. You take it from there!

SOLO 30, LETTER D

The syncopation in this 6/4 piece gives you unlimited opportunities for distributing these phrases on the drumset. Even though in my example I have placed the rolls on the snare, try them on the toms.

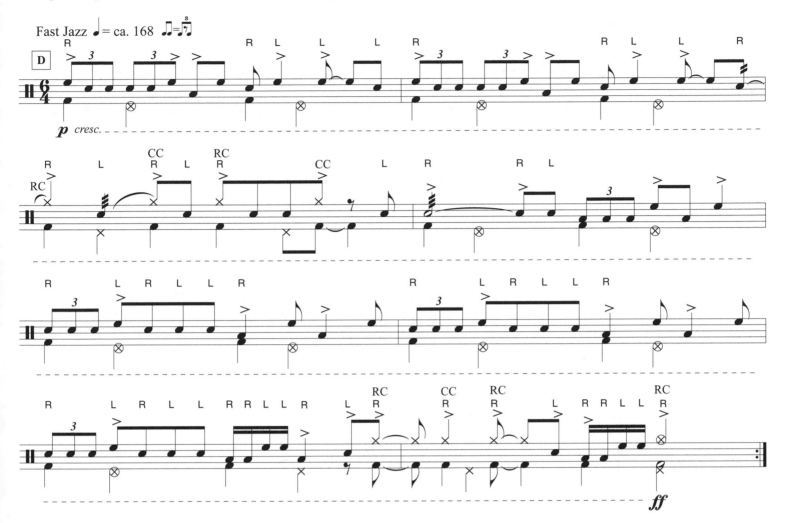

SOLO 31, LETTER A

Phrases in odd times like 9/4 can be challenging, as you have seen on the snare. Check what I've done as a guide and do your own thing. Always start with some time so you get that right feel.

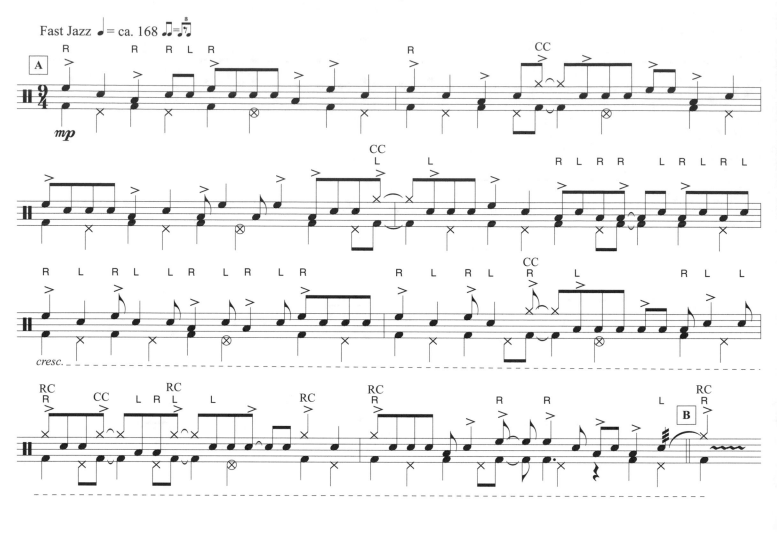

SOLO 36, LETTER B

Play straight eighths on this Latin phrase that I have provided from Solo 36. Work on your own drumset ideas. The change from Latin to swing is good practice for those situations you'll encounter in your ensemble work.

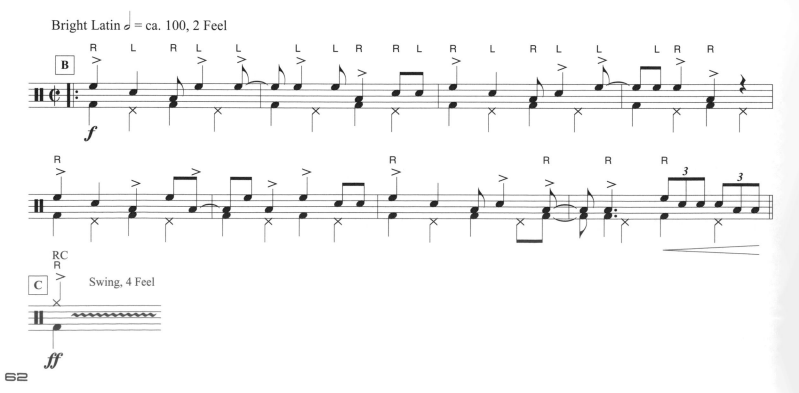

SOLO 38, LETTER E

Look at what I've done on the drumset with this up tempo, double-time and half-time phrase at E, and use it as inspiration for your own ideas. Solo 38 is a good one to practice to become secure transitioning between double time and half time.

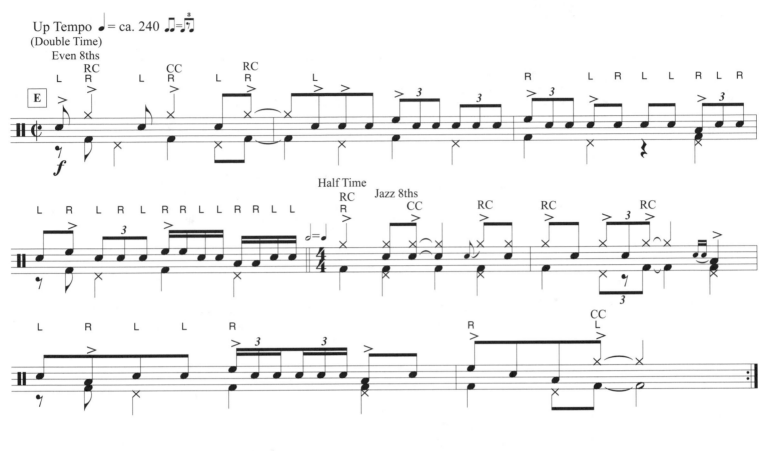

SOLO 45, LETTER C

Moving from 7/8 time (even eighths) to 4/4 time (jazz eighths) took some work to accomplish with the snare, and will take even more with the set! This example shows what I would do at C. It should help you with all of Solo 45 on the set. This kind of practice will prepare you for modern jazz and fusion. Have fun with these somewhat "different" licks.

SOLO 48, LETTER B

As you work out all of Solo 48 on the drumset, innumerable possibilities present themselves. With these changing meter phrases and licks under your belt, you will be able to solve just about any problem in this musical context.

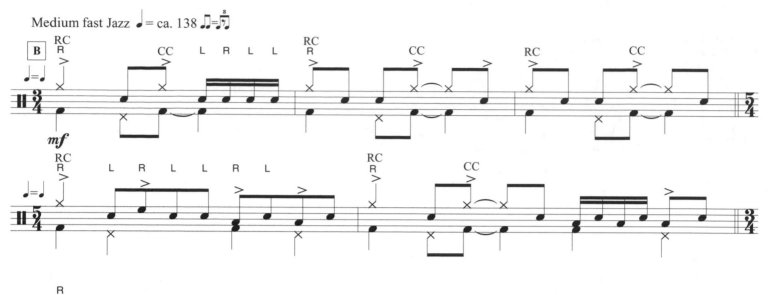

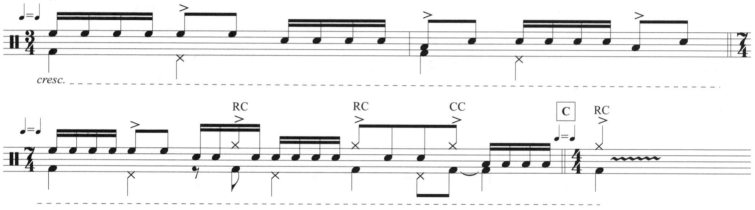

SOLO 50, LETTER A

Here is the beginning—letter A—of the last of the solos, Number 50. As you may remember from the snare drum, it's a busy piece, so getting around the set smoothly and easily will demand some careful planning and practice. You deserve a pat on the back when you've accomplished this—and, of course, the others—on the drumset. Congratulations!

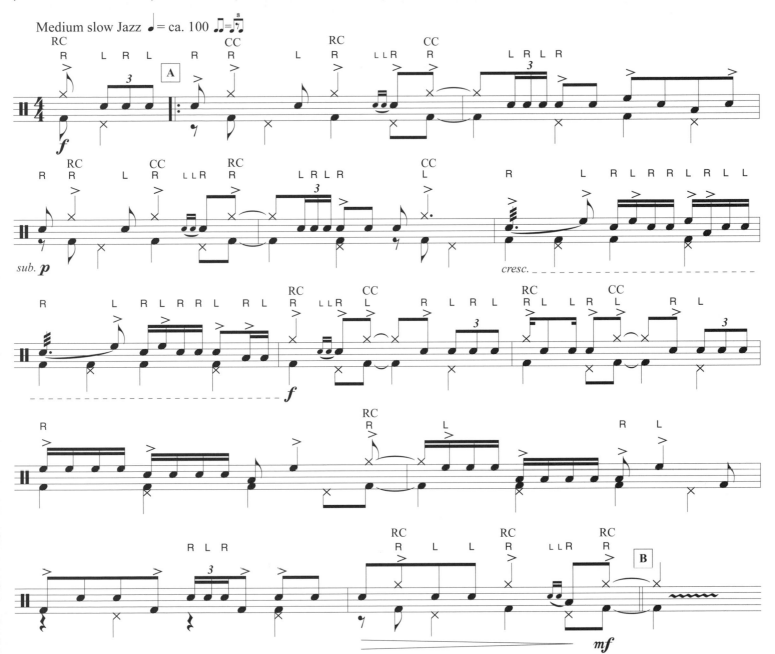

COMPING SNARE DRUM SOLOS

Comping the fifty syncopated snare drum solos provides an excellent opportunity to expand your independence and coordination horizons. The more difficult solos will present problems when comping, and you can, of course, elect to play them on the snare or set. Here's a tip for comping the complicated phrases and rolls: when you need both hands for the snare, start the phrase with the ride cymbal (which will give a semblance of time), play the hard lick, and then, when the music allows, you can return to the ride cymbal. The bass drum can help where it naturally fits into the lines you are playing. Use your imagination, and you'll be amazed at some of the phrases you'll come up with. Modern drummers use these ideas not only in comping, but in solos as well.

On pages 68–71, I have written out examples of how I would comp some of the solos. Here, as when playing the solos on the drumset, you have limitless possibilities. The more you experiment with your own ideas, the more inventive you will become, and fresh ideas will come to you more easily.

I think it is important for the proper musical feeling to play the solos again on either the snare or drumset before starting to comp them. Personally, it gives me insight and direction into which ways I can "travel."

Listening to the great drummers, and most definitely the modern ones, is a must and will certainly give you the motivation that you need.

Chops and coordination are certainly necessary, but remember your main goal and function should be to make music, which is the main idea throughout this whole book. Keep that it mind. Be conscious of your sound. Always listen carefully to each instrument and be critical. Don't settle for anything except your best.

As always, and as you hear me on the audio, begin the solos with some time.

Keep searching for new and different solutions. Enjoy the taste of mastering every new challenge!

EXAMPLE 1
Solo 2, Letter B, First Four Bars

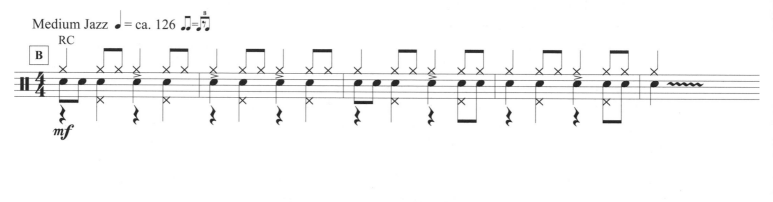

On this first comping example, I wrote the four bars at B for the left hand on the snare drum, while the right hand keeps time.

When you have mastered these first four bars, try the whole solo with just the left hand, keeping time with the right hand. After you are confident playing with the snare drum, add the bass drum as I did in the following examples.

Find the best solution that works for you. Don't be afraid to experiment with different combinations.

The tempo is just a guide. Start slowly and carefully. You can move the tempo up as you gain control.

Keep a nice sense of flowing time with the ride cymbal, and make those eighths swing/groove.

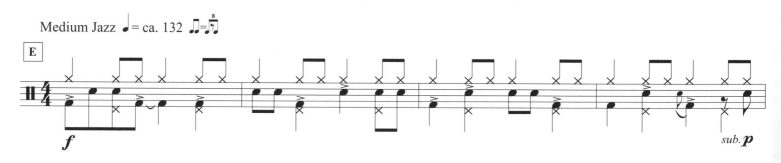

EXAMPLE 2
Solo 3, Letter E, First Four Bars

Beginning with this example, I am dividing the music line between the snare drum and the bass drum. I suggest that you also try that in Example 1.

Here is one way of orchestrating this phrase. Use what I've done, and play all of Solo 3 in this manner using your own ideas. Don't rush! Take your time and let your imagination lead you. Don't settle for one solution; go back and try other ways to comp the phrases.

EXAMPLE 3
Solo 4, Letter E, First Four Bars

Check out how I solved the problem with the roll in bar 4! Listen to your phrasing and keep it flowing. This kind of practice will give you that ease and facility that you certainly need for comping!

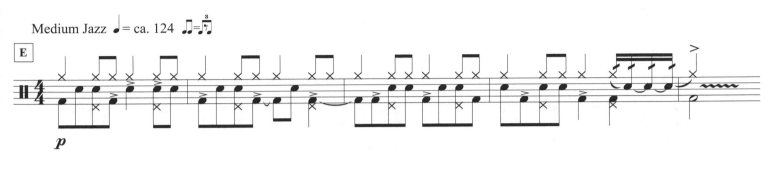

EXAMPLE 4
Solo 7, Letter E, First Four Bars

There are some triplets in this phrase, and they should fit nicely with the ride cymbal and eighth notes! The tempo markings are for playing the snare alone. You can of course base your comping on these tempos, but feel free to slow them down in the beginning, and then go on to a faster tempo later.

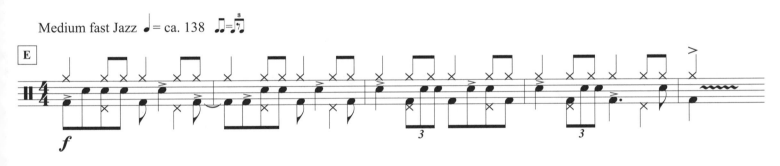

EXAMPLE 5
Solo 12, Letter D, First Four Bars

See how I used the flam, ruff, and sixteenth notes in this phrase. You might have a better idea. The main thing is to keep whatever you decide on moving with a good feel. This is not easy with the grace notes and sixteenths, but again, start slowly!

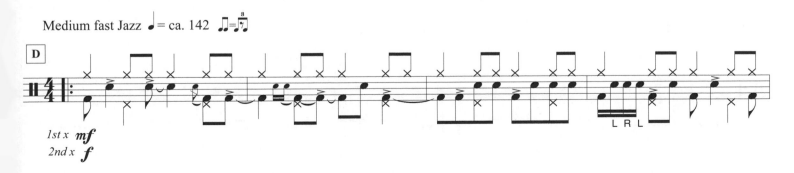

EXAMPLE 6
Solo 14, Letter B, First Four Bars

The flam in the first bar, the triplet sticking in the second bar, and the roll in the fourth bar require some practice. Again, this example is my way of working this out. You may have another solution. Working on this type of phrase will build and improve your accompanying skills.

EXAMPLE 7
Solo 23, Letter F, First Four Bars

This phrase is from one of the jazz waltz solos. Use the same approach as with the 4/4 solos except, of course, with the jazz waltz feel. Keep the notes between the bass drum and snare drum evenly distributed and make them swing/groove.

EXAMPLE 8
Solo 27, Letter C, First Four Bars

On to the 5/4 solos, where I have indicated a possible comping approach with the first four bars at C. You'll encounter 5/4 in modern jazz, and these syncopated solos will certainly prepare you for those musical situations. It goes without saying that feeling comfortable comping in 5/4 will give you a great advantage. Again, Example 8 shows my approach, but it's more important to incorporate your own ideas!

EXAMPLE 9
Solo 28, Letter A, First Four Bars

As you most certainly realized with the 7/4 solos, much concentrated practice is needed. Comping 7/4 will take some getting used to, but when you get the feel, you'll find 7/4 works quite naturally. Here I have indicated a comping possibility. This should help you get started. As I mentioned, some of the more complicated solos may not lend themselves to comping; try different sticking combinations and incorporating the ride cymbal, however it best fits the phrases, to keep the time feel going.

EXAMPLE 10
Solo 36, Letter E, First Four Bars

This last comping example has a Latin feel; it's played using straight eighths. Find the Latin groove that works best with the phrases you want to comp, and go from there. Again, you may need to change your groove from time to time depending on what phrases you need to comp. Practicing your comping to this solo and Solo 41 will give you the security and freedom you need when playing in the Latin idiom.

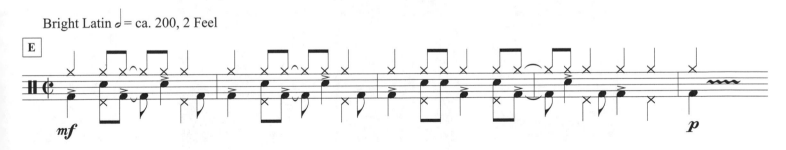

FOCUS ON FUNDAMENTALS
WITH HAL LEONARD SNARE DRUM BOOKS

HAL LEONARD SNARE DRUM METHOD

The Musical Approach to Snare Drum for Band and Orchestra

by Rick Mattingly

Geared toward beginning band and orchestra students, this modern, musical approach to learning snare drum includes a play-along CD that features full concert band recordings of band arrangements and classic marches with complete drum parts that allow the beginning drummer to apply the book's lessons in a realistic way. This book/CD pack also includes: fun-to-play solos and etudes; duets that can be played with another drummer, a teacher, or with the play-along tracks on the CD; studies in 4/4, 2/4, 3/4, 6/8 and cut-time; roll studies; and much more!

06620059 Book/CD Pack
.... $10.99

40 INTERMEDIATE SNARE DRUM SOLOS

by Ben Hans

This book is designed as a lesson supplement, or as performance material for recitals and solo competitions. Includes: 40 intermediate snare drum solos presented in easy-to-read notation; a music glossary; Percussive Arts Society rudiment chart; suggested sticking, dynamics and articulation markings; and much more!

06620067 .... $7.99

INNER RHYTHMS – MODERN STUDIES FOR SNARE DRUM

by Frank Colonnato

This intermediate to advanced-level book presents interesting and challenging etudes for snare drum based on the rhythms of contemporary music, including a variety of time signatures, shifting meters and a full range of dynamics. These studies will help improve reading skills as well as snare drum technique.

06620017 .... $7.95

SNARE DRUM PLAY-ALONG

by Joe Cox

This book has been designed to help intermediate and advanced drummers develop rudiment speed with play-along tracks that start slowly, accelerate, then slow back down. But what sets it apart from other rudiment books is musical grooves, in a number of different styles, which help the drummer to hear the sticking patterns. The melodies in the tracks mirror and/or compliment the left and right hands of the rudiment.

06620141 Book/CD Pack
.... $14.99

RUDIMENTAL DRUM SOLOS FOR THE MARCHING SNARE DRUMMER

by Ben Hans

Meant as a study for developing the rudiments in a musical manner, this book is designed as a progressive lesson supplement and as performance material for recitals, contests, and solo competitions. Includes: solos featuring N.A.R.D., P.A.S., and hybrid drum rudiments; warm-up exercises; and more.

06620074 .... $12.95

SNARE DRUM SOLOS

Seven Pieces for Concert Performance

by Sperie Karas

These solos provide excellent performance material for recitals and solo competition, and are perfect for use as lesson supplements. Seven solos include: The Fast Track • Hot News • Lay It Down • The Right Touch • Rollin' and Rockin' • Strollin' on Six • Waltz for Jazzers.

06620079 .... $5.95

THE 26 TRADITIONAL AMERICAN DRUMMING RUDIMENTS

by John S. Pratt

This collection of rudimental examples and roll charts will aid the learner in mastering the rudimental language. John S. Pratt's early works, now once again available, are an essential part of America's "traditional" drumming heritage. This new edition contains a new foreword and corrected music engravings, and also includes the classic solos "The Sons of Liberty" and "The All-American Emblem."

06620124 .... $9.99

128 RUDIMENTAL STREET BEATS, ROLLOFFS, AND PARADE-SONG PARTS

by John S. Pratt

This book contains "traditional" rudimental selections for snare, tenor, and bass drums that will provide the drum sections of parade or drilling units a varied repertoire of performance material. Contains a CD of the material performed by the author, helpful exercises for intermediate drummers, and a preface and foreword.

06620123 Book/CD Pack
.... $14.99

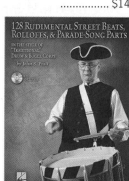

TRADITIONAL RUDIMENTAL DRUMMING

by John S. Pratt

In this DVD, John S. Pratt will reinvigorate your study of "traditional" ancient rudimental drumming and provide material for your practice, instruction, music library and drumming pleasure. The DVD includes: classic and new Pratt solos • four original Pratt compositions in the "Spirit of 1776" rope tension snare and bass drum duets with Ben Hans • printable scores on disc • and more.

00320825 DVD-ROM .. $24.99